Is There A Soul?

Madeline McNeill

Copyright © 2013 Madeline McNeill

All rights reserved.

ISBN-10: 148206605X
ISBN-13: 978-1482066050

Acknowledgements

I would like to thank Amanda Maule for her invaluable insight as editor extraordinaire. Thanks to Amaris Ketcham for the gorgeous cover design. And thanks to all my friends, family, and teachers, who have encouraged, guided, and supported me throughout my soul-searching endeavors

CONTENTS

Introduction	i
What is the meaning of life?	3
What are feelings?	7
What are emotions?	13
How do we think emotions?	18
How are emotions created?	22
Is there a soul?	31
What is creativity?	37
What is language?	42
How does meditation work?	47
What is consciousness?	51
What would a modern spirituality be?	56
What makes a person wise?	59

INTRODUCTION

    This book takes a modern slant on the form and philosophizing of ancient Greek dialogues. Instead of two men thinking abstractly, here, two women feel, using the body's musculature as the landscape for answering existential and philosophical questions. These women, a teacher and student, construct a two-sided conversation, exploring inner experience using trained muscle awareness.

    As the book progresses, the student learns how to become a practitioner of her teacher's theory, a body philosopher. Body philosophers are people who know how to reason through inner feelings and movements, and they move well. The teacher draws from years of studying math and sciences, the performing arts, and spiritual disciplines in order to answer each of the student's questions—What are feelings? What are emotions? Is there a soul? What makes a person wise?—among others. Together, they detail the structure of their core musculature through different emotional states, spiritual states, and states of mind. By methodically analyzing their inner-muscle sensations and processes of movement, they can gain insight into the human experience, and so can we.

    I organized the dialogues to gradually introduce theory while also casting a wide net. The goal is to lay the basic groundwork for a new way to explore philosophy. Because it takes time to internalize the theories, the dialogues should be read thoughtfully, and taking breaks is encouraged. The characters investigate the theory within their bodies, guiding the reader to do the same. The first five dialogues present new ideas and vocabulary. The next five, beginning with, "Is there a soul?" apply the theories to more complex concepts. The last two widen the lens to analyze cultural issues and suggest how to move forward with the theory and its application.

    Envisioning the application of this theory begins with thinking from the body. My ability to observe and analyze felt experience draws from years of study in opera, yoga, meditation, religions, and sciences. It points to a new way of theorizing that I believe women are poised to engage in. Women are generally more in tune with feelings in their bodies. With a growing number of women contributing to our intellectual institutions, it makes sense to expect that new theory exploring the nature of the mind will soon come from women exploring the nature of their own feeling intellect.

Student: What is the meaning of life?

Teacher: Why ask that question first?

S: Well, I figure if we're going to talk deeply, I may as well start with a question that puts everything into perspective. Why not start with the meaning of life?

T: It's a good question, but instead of focusing on the answer, try to focus on how the question is asked. Ask the question again, and as you ask, bring your attention to your body.

S: Bring attention to my body? I'm not sure what you mean. I'll try. "What's the meaning of life?" I don't really notice much in my body. For the most part, I'm calm.

T: Are you always calm when you ask the question?

S: No, I don't think so. Sometimes I may be frustrated.

T: How frustrated?

S: Just exasperated. With life.

T: How exasperated?

S: I don't know. I'm not wringing my hands at the sky. I guess I'm usually pretty calm when I think about the meaning of life. Maybe at the core I'm frustrated, but it doesn't manifest in a big way. It's a milder frustration.

T: That's good. Now let's form an equation starting with all the variables that go into asking the question.

S: Variables? Do you mean what's on my mind?

T: Yes.

S: It's not just the meaning of my life, but everyone's life, humanity's life.

T: Do you only mean people?

S: I know there are all kinds of life, but people are different. It seems as if we need things to mean something. Why is that? And if we need meaning, shouldn't we be able to figure out the meaning of life?

T: We can find meaning by structuring experience inwardly. Life is one big continuous experience, only lived once. A person asking, "What is the meaning of life," attempts to structure an experience that has not yet been fully experienced from beginning to end. People shouldn't stop trying to find meaning in life, but they should understand the limitations involved in asking the question.

In order to structure experience inwardly, observe how you ask the question by considering what you think and what you feel. Conceptually, human beings have the ability to think several thoughts in a few moments. As you ask the question, you remember experiences you have had and things you have read, heard, or seen about peoples' lives and call that "life." So you conceptualize "life" from a few moments of thought experiences. Then you assign that word a felt emotion: mild frustration.

S: Is that bad?

T: No, it just is. That's how the question is asked. What happens to your breath when you ask a question that you want an answer to right away? Say you ask someone for the time.

S: I ask the question, "What time is it?" I hold my breath.

T: You suspend your breath until the person answers your question. You begin breathing again when the person gives you the answer.

S: Why do I do that?

T: You relinquish your breath to someone else. You trust that person to give you your next breath by answering your question. The interaction demonstrates an unconscious body language.

S: But I didn't hold my breath when I asked, "What is the meaning of life?"

T: You're right. Why didn't you?

S: I don't know. I'd probably pass out if I did. I wouldn't get an answer soon enough to breathe again.

T: Exactly. You asked the question with a moan.

S: A moan?

T: Frustration.

S: Frustration is a moan?

T: A subtle moan. Why do you moan?

S: To express pain. Sadness. Frustration, too.

T: Yes. And where is the moan in the body?

S: What do mean, "Where is it?"

T: Where is it generated? Do you feel a moan deep in your body?

S: Yeah, I'd say I feel it deeply.

T: Consider what you conceptualized when you asked, "What is the meaning of life," and what you felt in your breath. Which was more real, your momentary conceptualization of the term "life" or the moan that asked the question?

S: My conceptualization of "life" was a pretty inaccurate representation, but the moan was real.

T: Do you feel that as true?

S: I do. It's just very blunt.

T: It is, but it also nicely defines things. We've just broken down the question into two variables: what is conceptualized, and what is felt. In addition to the thoughts a question provokes, we should observe what we feel when we ask the question in order to answer it.

S: But I still don't know how to answer the question.

T: We find meaning by structuring inner experience. Asking, "What is the meaning of life," is an experience in itself. Now that you understand more about the experience of asking the question, can you imagine a better way to approach it?

S: Well, I could imagine more of life when I think about the question, or I could try to think longer about everything involved in life to represent the concept better.

T: Those are good ways to approach the question, though a person couldn't possibly imagine it all. Perhaps you could try a different approach.

S: What would that be?

T: You could learn to structure your moan.

S: What are feelings?

T: Do you mean emotional feelings in the core?

S: Emotional, yes, but what's the core?

T: Think of the core as the torso, neck, and head, or the body without the arms and legs. We'll mostly focus on the deeper muscles of the core, the muscles that breathe and speak and move emotionally. I'd like you to bring your awareness into your core. Give attention to these locations as I say them: the muscles of the face and inside the mouth, the lips, tongue, and soft palate. The neck and throat. The shoulders, chest, and upper back. Around the ribs. The domed diaphragm under the lungs. The layers of muscle around the abdomen. The muscles of the lower back. Within the pelvis. And finally, the organ musculature of the gut, the stomach, and up to the heart. These are a few of the core muscles that can be felt, some with more clarity than others. We can feel our core muscles even if we can't see them.

S: But what do core muscles have to do with feelings?

T: What do you think emotional feelings are?

S: They say the brain controls feelings.

T: What do you think about that?

S: I'm not sure…. It doesn't feel right to me. Feelings seem more than messages sent from the brain to the body. What do you think? Am I being naïve?

T: No. You're being perceptive. Try a different approach. Try to imagine what you feel as experiences of sensory muscles.

S: Sensory muscles? How are muscles sensory?

T: Let's start with a familiar muscle experience. Do you play sports?

S: I run.

T: Do your leg muscles get tired after a hard run?

S: Yeah.

T: Do your leg muscles feel tired after a hard run?

S: What's the difference?

T: Getting tired is the muscle event. Feeling tired is muscle sensing the event. Muscles are essential to the felt sense, or more specifically, muscles are a sensory terrain for feeling.

S: What do you mean by sensory terrain?

T: Think of the senses: sight, hearing, smell, taste, and touch. They all need three components to work: a sensory terrain, nerves, and the brain. All sensory terrains are structures of sensory tissue—flesh designed to gather sensory information in conjunction with nerves. The skin is sensory terrain for touch, and the eyes are sensory terrain for sight. In the same way, muscles are sensory terrain for feeling from inside the body.
    Let's approach it another way. Consider deeply felt experiences. All people have deep experiences that they feel in their bodies. The question is, how do people explain these experiences?

S: Some people talk about soul or energy or spirit. Some people talk about the brain and nerves in control. Then, there are hormones.

T: Do you think any of those could be considered a sensory terrain?

S: No. I don't think about any sensory terrain when I think about feeling.

T: So, from your perspective, there is no specified sensory terrain for feeling. That could mean one of two things: either no felt sense exists because no sensory terrain exists; or, because we don't acknowledge a sensory terrain, we assume no felt sense exists.

S: So, which one is it?

T: The second. We don't conceptualize our feelings as part of a sensory process because we don't conceptualize a sensory terrain for feeling. By acknowledging muscles as a sensory terrain, feeling becomes a sensory process.

S: But what exactly do the muscles feel?

T: The muscles feel many kinds of sensations including temperature, pressure, contraction, pain, release, rejuvenation, relaxation, and fatigue.

It will make it easier to understand by moving through an example. I want you to put your hand behind your head. Without moving your hand or looking at it, I want you to describe its orientation to me. Describe it as if I were going to draw a picture of your hand solely based on your description.

S: Okay. My palm is facing down but also angled slightly away from my head. My fingers are bent a little, maybe an inch apart at the tips. My thumb is parallel to my pointer finger. How's that?

T: That's good. Sensory awareness of movement is called proprioception. The muscles have the ability to feel their own orientation and movement by feeling sensations of muscle contraction. The degree of detail depends on your own sensory ability. Let's take it a step further and see how much detail you can describe to train your sensory ability. Bring further awareness into your hand, focusing specifically on muscular sensations of the fingers. In which finger do you feel the strongest muscle contraction?

S: My pinky has the most contraction.

T: And where exactly do you feel the contraction in your pinky?

S: I feel it on top, between the second and third joints, and I feel a kind of pressure in the tip and the outside of the pinky going all the way to my palm.

T: Good. You can rest your hand. You just moved through an exercise bringing detailed awareness to your muscles using only the muscles' ability to feel contraction sensations. It was necessary to take your eyesight out of the equation to prove muscles can gather sensory information without needing the other senses. Muscles continuously feel their own state of being.

S: But why can't I say that the nerves feel the state of being of the muscles?

T: You could, as long as you acknowledge that the nerves wouldn't be feeling much of anything if the muscles weren't there. Muscles provide the landscape for inner events to be felt. Nerves innervate the muscle. Muscle is feeling flesh, like skin is feeling flesh. I'll put it this way: what if a person had no skin and only nerve endings?

S: That's gross. You're talking about a skinless person with just nerve endings? The person wouldn't last very long.

T: And they certainly couldn't exercise the sense of touch. The skin is flesh designed to gather sensory information. The same comparison applies to muscles. Muscles are feeling flesh. They feel sensations. They also initiate sensations.

S: How do they do that?

T: There are a few ways muscle can initiate sensation in the body. Muscle tension can initiate sensation. For example, most people have experienced a headache. Often, a headache stems from muscle tension. Tension from the trapezius muscle can refer pain in the temple, behind the eye, or around the ear.
    We'll bring this experience into the body. I'll find my trapezius muscle, this roll of muscle where the neck meets the shoulder, and feel for muscle tension. When I find a knot, I massage it between my thumb and forefinger. As I massage, I distinctly feel referred pain in my temple. The knot itself feels like a taut band beneath the skin. By massaging it directly, the muscle refers pain.

S: I'm trying, but I can't find anything.

T: It takes time to become skilled at feeling for muscle tension. Let me help you find tension in your trapezius. I'll start with gentle pressure as I search out a knot in your trapezius with my fingers. I'm rolling the muscle between my fingers searching for muscle tissue that feels hard and constricted, like a taut band or bead beneath the skin. Because muscles are three-dimensional, sometimes a knot needs to be approached from different sides or even from underneath. Here's one. I'll massage the knot gradually increasing the pressure, and as I do, I want you to feel for referred pain higher in your neck and head.

S: Okay. I feel referred pain in the back of my neck, and behind my ear.

T: Try it yourself. Bring your thumb and forefinger to the place where my hand is. Do you feel the knot?

S: Yeah. It feels like a stiff cord.

T: Now roll the knot slowly between your fingers, gradually increasing pressure while feeling for referred pain in your neck and head.

S: Oh yeah. I definitely feel that. It's really strong behind my ear. That's crazy. So, what's happening? Why is there referred pain?

T: For now, acknowledge that what you just experienced was referred pain caused by muscle tension. It's one of the many ways that muscles initiate an experience of sensation within the body.

S: I have to admit, part of me doesn't want to think of muscles initiating sensation. I imagine them moving according to what they are told to do.

T: That's because you're imagining a system where muscles are submissive instead of sensory. It may help you understand your muscles as sensory if you practice defining inner sensations as muscle experiences. Let's practice how this works by moving through another example, this time more centered in the core. Bring your attention to your throat. Contract your larynx as if there is a "lump in your throat." Feel those sensations in detail. What does it feel like?

S: It feels like a constriction in my throat. Like a clenching that goes into my tongue.

T: That's good. The throat is lined with muscle tissue. A "lump in the throat" describes the felt experience of muscle contraction in the larynx. When life throws you an experience causing you to have a "lump in the throat," all kinds of factors like hormones or memories may influence the muscle contraction, but the felt experience is still a muscle experience.

S: But it still seems to me that when I feel emotionally, there's more going on. It feels deeper than what muscles can feel.

T: Can you explain more of what you mean?

S: I may feel love in my heart. Or I'll get a gut feeling. Or I'll have a nervous stomach.

T: That's true. What you describe are literally deep core feelings felt by muscular organs.

S: What do organs have to do with muscles?

T: Those three organs you just mentioned—the gut, the stomach, and the heart—all have muscle tissue. Cardiac muscle in the heart circulates blood through the body. Smooth muscle in the stomach and gut digest and transport food through the body. The muscular nature of these organs defines their purpose as organs meant to move substantive solids and fluids through the body. They serve a purpose through their muscular movement, which groups them as part of the core musculature.

I want to reiterate my point regarding the full purpose of all muscles: not only do muscles move, they also feel. This idea explains why we reference the heart, stomach, and gut when we talk about feelings. These organ muscles, like skeletal muscles, are meant to feel the environment within the body as well as their own states of being. For example, the heart may beat fast or slow. It can feel cold or warm. It can feel free, or heavy, or even "broken." These experiences suggest that the heart muscle feels as it moves. You could think of it as muscle terrain continuously interacting with changes in its environment.

All core muscles, from the deepest organs to those surrounding them, continuously experience sensation. The experiences of the core muscles compose our most profound felt experiences. We can learn to map and analyze deeply felt experience, but it takes practice and knowledge of one's own core musculature. You have to learn to understand the rules and nature of sensation, the shapes of the core muscles, as well as how to feel processes of movement over time.

S: That all sounds like it's hard to do.

T: It is. Core muscles have complex behaviors, varying terrains, and unique ways of moving. Mapping them begins with imagining your core muscles as experiencers of sensation: the stomach musculature feeling cramping pain, jaw muscles feeling tension, muscles in the throat feeling pressure, the heart feeling warmth, the diaphragm and abdominals feeling their own breathing movement. Sometimes muscles create the sensation, as you experienced with the referred pain. A range of core muscle experience can be felt in detail, like your experience of feeling detailed sensations in your pinky finger.

The trick to understanding all of this begins with approaching the inquiry correctly. We must revisit the body, feeling first, and then conceptualize what is felt with a vocabulary created for the sensory musculature.

S: What are emotions?

T: Emotions are structured experiences that are felt in the core.

S: What does that mean?

T: If there was a difference between emotions and feelings, how would you describe it?

S: I don't know. When I talk about feelings, I might say something like, "You hurt my feelings," or "I have feelings for someone." When I talk about emotions, I describe how I'm feeling as in, "I'm sad," or "I'm happy."

T: Are feelings more difficult to describe than emotions?

S: Yeah, maybe feelings are more random, and emotions have more purpose. Does that make sense?

T: That's a good start. Let's talk about locations of feelings. Where do you feel them?

S: I know feelings are in the core, but when I talk about my personal feelings, I'm mostly talking about what I feel below my head.

T: Why not in the head?

S: I don't know. I don't really know what's happening below my head.

T: Let's get below the head by moving through an example. We'll divide feelings into what feels good and what feels bad and map the feelings in the body. We'll start with the bad, or more specifically, pain. Imagine pain in your body. What does it feel like?

S: I think pain can feel like a lot of things. It depends. It might feel like an ache or a burning in my body, sometimes intense, like a shock even. But I don't know if all pain is bad.

T: You're right. Pain is part of life. Pain can also be instructive if you know how to pay attention to it. How about sensations that feel good, how would you describe those?

S: I don't know, maybe warm or like a nice ache or a tickle.

T: Where?

S: It can feel good in lots of places.

T: In the chest?

S: Yeah.

T: How about the stomach?

S: Yeah.

T: Pelvis?

S: Um, of course.

T: Can it feel good in the face and neck?

S: I don't know. Does a smile feel good? I'm not sure about that. I associate the face and neck more with where the feelings are expressed.

T: Good. Now the conversation begins to turn to emotion.

S: Are you saying that feelings in the body are expressed in the face, and that's emotion?

T: No, but you've touched on the central point. Emotions are structured events, whereas feelings lack structure.

S: Feelings lack structure. What do you mean?

T: You said earlier that feelings seem random. That was a good observation. Consider the idea that feelings are or at least feel like random events in the core, whereas emotions feel like structured events. We'll explore this idea by mapping an emotion. We'll map it by defining where it is felt throughout the core. Can you name a strong emotion?

S: How about anger?

T: That's a great example. Create anger in yourself. Take yourself into an argument you had with someone in the past until you can start feeling the sensations of anger. Can you do that?

S: Yeah, I think so.

T: Where do you feel anger?

S: I think… I feel anger strongly in my throat, like a hot clenching.

T: What else?

S: I feel more hot clenching below my sternum and in my gut.

T: What do you feel in your face?

S: My eyebrows furrow.

T: You've just mapped and described several locations and sensations of anger. The next step is to analyze the map. When you are angry, are the contraction locations in the front of the core or the back?

S: If I had to choose, I think they're mostly in the front. If I contract in the back of my body too, that's like being both scared and angry, but pure anger seems to be mostly in the front.

T: I can feel what you mean about being scared. That's a good observation. So, the core posture of anger forms a contraction pattern mainly at the front of the body.

S: The core posture?

T: A core posture is a pose of the core muscles. It positions the core muscles like a moving architecture, creating a pattern of sensations felt throughout the torso, neck, and head.

S: You said it's a pose. What do you mean by pose?

T: Have you ever done yoga?

S: Yeah.

T: In yoga you move into different yoga poses with the entire body. A core posture poses the core muscles only. It's like a yoga pose or a dance pose but relegated to the core musculature.

S: We mapped the core posture of anger?

T: A general mapping, yes. Anger is a structured event in the core, a core posture characterized by the feelings you described at specific places in the body.

S: That's interesting.

T: What do you find interesting?

S: The idea of core postures.

T: Each emotion has its own. They can all be mapped like we just did with anger. The trick to mapping a core posture is learning to feel its entire structure throughout the core.

S: Feel its entire structure? That sounds hard to do.

T: It can be. To feel the entire structure, you have to feel in multiple places at the same time. It's a skill to feel each emotion's entire organized pattern of felt sensations in order to distinguish one emotion from another.

S: Not everyone would be good at that, right? It seems like it would be hard for some people to do.

T: That's true. An emotionally skilled person can move through core postures while feeling the sensations of each core posture with detail and clarity.

S: That sounds really physical.

T: It is. Emotions should be approached and studied in a very physical way by people who move flexibly in their core, who can skillfully feel in their core, and can intelligently analyze processes of felt movement by tracking sensation patterns over time. For them, feeling would be a legitimate tool for gathering information about core experience.

S: You mean they would feel in order to find their answers?

T: They would feel, map, analyze, and then find ways to corroborate their felt analysis with other means of scientific observation. But from the very beginning, the inquiry must be approached correctly. Emotions are structured events experienced by the core musculature. Investigating emotions begins with moving through and mapping them in one's own body.

S: How do we think emotions?

T: Do you like to think?

S: Yeah, I like to think a lot.

T: Why?

S: It's what I do. I'll daydream, put myself in scenarios, and have imaginary conversations. It's the best when I have a comfortable chair, and I can sit in the sun, look out the window, and let my mind wander. I like it.

T: So, it feels good.

S: Yeah. I don't think of thinking as feeling good, but I feel good when I do it.

T: Would you say you're an internal person?

S: Definitely. I enjoy being by myself. Not all the time, of course. I like people, but I don't say a whole lot. The thing is, I don't feel quiet. Does that make sense? I don't say much, but I don't feel quiet.

T: It does make sense. Thinking includes core movement, though the movement is often very subtle. For example, when a person talks to herself, she still speaks, but with muscle engagement so subtle that no sound comes out. She is subtly posturing, or subposturing her words and emotions. A person subposturing emotion moves from one emotional core posture to the next, but the movement can be so subtle, it's imperceptible. It's part of a spectrum of how intensely a person engages the core musculature. Sometimes people feel most comfortable engaging dynamically, while others prefer to engage subtly.

S: Then I feel more comfortable engaging subtly?

T: It's possible. Think of how people move through core postures differently. Some people move dynamically from one core posture to another. They would be the emotionally outgoing people.

S: They would be extroverted.

T: Yes, but designating people as extroverted and introverted isn't the best way to understand personality. There is too much diversity among "extroverted" people to lump them all together. For example, one person may be an outgoing, emotionally dynamic singer moving skillfully from one core posture to another, while another person might be loud, but may not be able to move between core postures.

S: What do you mean, they "may not be able to move between core postures"?

T: Think of it this way. Imagine a person who speaks emphatically with one emotion, never varying. Say they express anger loudly and all of the time, or disgust all the time, or ecstatic happiness all the time.

S: I'm imagining a pulpit pounding preacher.

T: That's a good example.

S: I feel with them it's one long shout of God babble.

T: It can be tiring.

S: What does it mean if the preacher guy speaks with just one emotion?

T: Try to answer the question knowing that each emotion has its own core posture.

S: Would he be speaking with only one core posture?

T: Yes.

S: Why?

T: There could be many reasons. Maybe he doesn't know how to engage many other core postures of emotion.

S: Ha. He doesn't know how. I don't know why, but that's funny to me. It makes him sound unintelligent with his emotions. It also makes me think of sports, like an emotional linebacker who barrels through, and that's all he can do. Okay, I'm definitely not like that. I mean I'm not really quiet, but I'm not that energetic either. I think I can move through many core postures, but I'm not always outgoing with my emotions, so what's that?

T: I would say you subposture with sophistication.

S: That sounds like a compliment. What exactly does that mean?

T: It means you intelligently move through subtle core postures as you think.

S: And that's good?

T: Yes. You subtly engage complex core postures of emotion and speech but so subtly that you produce no sound.

S: I'm still not sure what you mean when you say I produce no sound. How does that work?

T: To answer that question, you'll have to think of how muscles can move between robust and subtle contraction. Muscles contract with varying degrees of intensity. To make the explanation simpler, let's get out of the core for a second. We'll move through an example of lifting the leg.
   Right now we are both sitting down. Our legs are mostly in a state of rest. Let's both lift the right leg a few inches from the floor. Now, put it down. Now, without actually lifting the leg, subtly engage those same muscles you used to lift it before. The goal is to subtly contract and coordinate muscles that lifted the leg, and feel them contracting without actually lifting the leg. This is an example of subtle, structured muscle movement. The muscle coordination would lift the leg, but the muscle contraction was too subtle to fully carry out the activity. It's the same idea with core postures through the musculature of the core. We can robustly engage core postures by robustly engaging the core muscles, or we can subtly engage core postures to subposture where the movement is not perceptible.

S: Perceptible by who?

T: Others don't notice it, and you might not acknowledge it. Thought includes subposturing. You talk or emote to yourself without producing sound. The core posture movement becomes so subtle, it can become imperceptible.

S: You're saying when I'm talking to myself, I'm still moving from one subtle core posture to another. I'm still moving in my core when I think?

T: That's right. Subtly moving and emoting.

S: That's cool. I subposture when I think. What does that say about my personality?

T: It suggests that your core muscles feel comfortable with complex, subtle core posture movement.

S: I like to subposture. I'm still emoting; it's just subtle. Hm. I guess I can never be like a pulpit pounding preacher.

T: That's just fine. Better to be an emotionally intelligent person.

S: How are emotions created?

T: What are your thoughts about it?

S: You talked about how emotions are structured, but does that mean they are structured from the brain? I ask because part of me doesn't want to believe they are created in the brain, especially now. That doesn't seem right to me. It doesn't feel right.

T: It doesn't feel right, but it seems you're not sure how to counter the argument.

S: Right. All I know is it doesn't feel right that emotions only come from the head. It makes everything seem predetermined, like I have no control. Isn't that funny, that I say "I have no control" when "I" supposedly comes from the brain, too? It drives me nuts. It makes me feel like someone is trying to convince me that the rest of my body doesn't matter, like it's a marionette for the brain. The brain is so isolated. Does that sound dumb?

T: Not at all. I agree with you.

S: So, you don't think emotions come from the brain?

T: No.

S: Do they come from the core?

T: Sometimes. Don't think of emotions originating from one place every time. Try to imagine a dialogue between the brain and core as the emotion structures itself.

S: How would that work?

T: It might be easier to start by critically examining the current paradigm. When it comes to complex events like emotions, we think that the brain and nervous system command the body, or more exact to our discussion, the brain and nerves command muscle. In other words, we have become very used to thinking muscles play a submissive role until they are told what to do, but that isn't the reality. First of all, muscles are sensory, working in conjunction with the nervous system to gather sensations. By accepting muscles as part of a sensory system, it becomes much easier to conceptualize a dialogue between feeling muscle and the brain instead of a one-way process with the brain in sole control. With a dialogue in mind, we can begin to explore how muscle contributes to the dialogue, which leads me to an important point.

Muscles actually initiate muscle activity independently of the brain. A simple example is a reflex. Though people often conceptualize reflexes as nerve controlled reactions, consider the idea that muscle movement initiates reflex activity. You've experienced this when the doctor performs the patellar reflex test or the knee-jerk test, where the little hammer strikes below the knee and there is a reflex kick movement. The hammer strikes the patellar tendon which causes a muscle in the lower thigh to stretch. The stretching muscle is in a different location than the original hammer strike. This act of stretching muscle stimulates the nervous system, which then stimulates contraction of the same muscle in the thigh. The leg kicks, and it was the muscle stretch that initialized the reflex.

S: The hammer doesn't hit a nerve causing the leg to kick?

T: No. The hammer strike caused a muscle in another location to stretch, and that stretch stimulated the nerve. The muscle activity initiated reflex activity. Direct nerve stimulation can initiate reflex too, but it's important to remember that nerves are part of the muscle sense, just like nerves are part of the skin sense. When we think about the sense of touch, we think of the skin, not the nerves. It should be the same with the muscle sense.

S: We've focused too much on nerves?

T: Yes. Remember the muscles as a sensory terrain with nerves innervating the muscle. With this approach, we can start to discover and analyze everything the sensory muscles do, which is true for core muscles as well. Core muscles have a rich sensory character, and they can also initiate reflex activity. Moving forward with this idea, we can begin to discuss how emotions are partially organized by core muscles.

S: Emotions are organized by the core? You mean independently of the brain?

T: Yes. The core muscles actively contribute to the creation of core postures, to the creation of emotions. The reasoning can be observed in the body. A simple core posture forms when a core muscle contraction in one location of the body stimulates multiple, simultaneous reflex contractions throughout the core. I call them inter-core reflexes. A simple example is a cough. A cough can begin with an irritation in the throat, which immediately stimulates contraction of the throat muscles. The throat muscle contraction then stimulates the nervous system to distribute reflex contraction throughout the entire core.

S: <cough> Okay, so, a person feels a tickle in their throat and that initiates a cough reflex?

T: Yes. Imagine a sequence of muscle contractions. A muscle contracts in one area, triggering reflex pathways, which then stimulate other muscles throughout the core to contract. A cough begins in the throat and then quickly becomes a full core event with contraction throughout the torso, neck, and head. To analyze a cough, let's actually subdivide the core into six areas: the head, neck, upper-torso, mid-torso, low-torso, and pelvis. Practice the cough and try to feel contraction in each area. Then tell me where you feel the contraction.

S: A cough analysis. Here we go. <cough, cough> In my head, I feel a contraction in the tongue, and the face, <cough> in the top front of my neck, and deeper down in my throat, <cough, cough> a little contraction in the chest, <cough> a lot below the sternum, <cough> belly and back contraction, <cough> and there's some in the pelvis too, right?

T: Excellent, your skills of self-observation are very good. Having moved through that example, does it make sense that the coordinated movements of coughing involve inter-core reflexes engaging muscles in those six areas of the core?

S: I get the idea. The locations remind me of the chakras.

T: That's true. It's no coincidence that the core locations we are focusing on are similar to the chakra locations.

S: Why? Are chakras real?

T: The chakra experience is real. Chakras were conceptualized before people had a detailed understanding of the anatomy and physiology of the body, so they theorized about what they felt based on available information. They came up with the idea that energy centers influence emotions, breath, and mind. We are at the point now we can scientifically disprove energy centers as major substantive entities, but we can't disprove the experience of people who feel chakras.

For investigators today, the solution is to theorize about these felt experiences with a modern, scientific approach. First, we should notice that people imagine chakras having substance. In other words, the people who conceptualized chakras conceptualized a physical energy terrain. So the question is: can we conceptualize a biological terrain that explains the chakra experience as people feel it? Is it just nerves? No, because nerves don't exist in a vacuum; they need a tissue structure to innervate. Hormones don't fit because hormones travel to a tissue structure to chemically affect it. What is "it" then that is innervated and affected, that feels intelligent in how it responds to the changes in the inner environment? Core muscles have a valid claim as long as they are acknowledged as a sensory terrain. Once they're fully acknowledged, we can begin to define the experience of chakras in a new way.

S: You're saying I could study the chakra experience using the techniques that you're teaching me?

T: Yes, I'm teaching you a new way to understand the science of felt experience. Throughout history people have worked to understand the mysteries of their felt experiences. Their theories became religions, spiritualties, and philosophies of thought. However, we are at a unique time when the old theories are rapidly and abundantly being disproved, creating a widespread need for new theory. By defining the characteristics of the sensory core musculature, we are filling a conceptual void. People are ready to examine felt experience with a vocabulary developed for the sensory musculature, but it has to begin with being able to observe and analyze what you feel within yourself. Let's get back to inter-core reflexes and move through an example in the body for practice. Let's try the core posture process of a moan. Do you remember where the moan is initiated?

S: That's when we were talking about the meaning of life, right? Was it deep in the body?

T: That's right. The moan can be conceptualized like a cough. Both demonstrate a process where an initial contraction stimulates a reflex pattern of contraction in the core. The initiation locations, however, are different. The cough initiates from the throat, whereas the moan initiates from the lower body.

S: I understand why the cough initiates from the throat, but I don't understand why the moan starts in the lower body.

T: Let's take a very clear example of pain. Say a person has indigestion. Where does the pain initiate?

S: It's in the gut.

T: Yes. The pain affects the smooth muscles of the intestine and the muscles in the low belly causing them to contract, which stimulates inter-core reflexes. When the gut contracts, it initiates inter-core reflexes in the stomach, the front of the diaphragm, the lower larynx, vocal cords, and then up into the head between the ears. Initiated from the gut, inter-core reflexes structure a core posture process: an exhaled moan with the core creating an inner shape so that as air passes through the vocal cords, the sound resonates in the space created within. That's the moan you hear. It will make more sense as you move through an example. Try to map the contraction locations of the moan.

S: Does that mean I have to moan to figure it out?

T: Yes, and it will have to be done authentically. Initiate it strongly in your lower abdomen with a strong muscle contraction on the exhale, then feel the different locations of inter-core reflex contractions throughout your core.

S: Okay <moan> It's initiated in the belly. I feel it in the pelvis, too.

T: Good. Don't be afraid of it. Just think that it's for scientific purposes.

S: Right, I'm moaning for science. <MOAN> That was a good one. I feel it below the sternum, a little in the chest, and in my throat.

T: Anything happening in the mouth and in the face?

S: <moan> Yeah. My mouth opens.

T: Anything else?

S: My tongue contracts. And I feel some contraction in my lips and my eyes.

T: You just moved through an example mapping an emotional expression as it structures in your core. In the case of the moan, the initiation is in the gut. From there, other muscles in the core contract, coordinated by inter-core reflexes.

S: But what's the purpose of inter-core reflexes?

T: They have many purposes. During the moan, the inter-core reflexes structure the core for communication. For example, say a young child has indigestion. As a parent, how would you know?

S: He would moan or cry.

T: The sound of the moan or cry is part of a structured expression—a core posture process initiated from the gut. If you heard your child moaning, you would empathize by subtly mimicking the core posture based on the sound of the child's moan.

S: I would mimic the core posture. I would moan, too?

T: Yes. You would subposture the moan mimicking what you hear and what you see. Expression on the child's face shows part of the entire core posture—the part you can see. By both seeing and hearing the moan you would gather information about the child's experience of pain.

S: You said I see the core posture in the face, but that's the only part of the core posture I see?

T: Yes. You can't actually see the indigestion, but you can see the core posture of pain structured by inter-core reflexes with the face being the most clearly observable part of the core posture.

We have all experienced indigestion, but if someone else is experiencing indigestion, the most we can do to feel their experience is to observe them and mimic their core posture. The facial contraction is the part you can see in another person, and the exhaled moan is the part you can hear. You gather information about their felt experience based on what you can see and hear, and with that information, you subposture a similar "moan" pattern within yourself. Then you analyze your experience by feeling the entire core posture within yourself.

Remember when you could feel the orientation of your hand when you put it behind your head? You couldn't see the orientation of your hand, but you could feel it. In the case of empathizing with a child's experience of indigestion, you observe the child's moan, you subposture the moan within yourself, then you feel the entire core posture of the moan which includes contractions and sensations in the lower body.

S: It does sound like a kind of wordless communication.

T: Communication with the core musculature. Whatever the cause for the initial "moan" muscle contraction, be it indigestion or sudden pressure to the gut or a rush of hormones, what follows is complex core activity for structuring the core posture, independent of brain participation. Of course, the brain participates in the structuring process, too, but my point is that the core has its own mechanisms that structure our emotions. Therefore, the core muscles play an essential role in how emotions are created. So far, we have been discussing simple examples, how inter-core reflexes structure very simple core-posture expressions like the cough and the moan. It starts to get really interesting when you apply the idea to more sophisticated expressions like speaking or singing.

S: What do you mean? How does it apply to singing?

T: Think again about the moan. Remember how it felt in the body and what a powerful expression it was. Singing can be equally powerful—more sophisticated of course—but the purpose of the moan and the purpose of singing a moan can be very similar. Both communicate information about the environment within the body. A moan demonstrates a structured event that can be caused by a deep hurt. A moan sings the blues. Have you ever seen a good blues singer?

S: It's been a while. I saw a live blues singer years ago. She was good. I really felt the emotion of her voice.

T: What made her singing authentic to you?

S: She seemed to be deep in her body, unafraid to express pain and sadness, but she could do it really musically.

T: Did you hear moaning in her singing?

S: Yeah, moans. They were strong sometimes, and other times they were subtle and sad. She could kill the audience with a quiet note, but it was so full of feeling. I was pretty blown away. How do singers do that?

T: Many singers can posture a range of emotion in addition to being able to posture pitch, rhythm, and vocal style. It sounds like the blues singer you heard could powerfully posture emotion from low in her core. She could sing a moan with nuanced sophistication and raw strength. In order to do that, singers have to feel not only detailed sensations, but the pathways of inter-core reflex activity. Inter-core reflexes create the experience of something moving through the core. They create a felt domino effect of contraction and sensation. Learning to feel contractions and sensations predominates voice training. Of course, singers might not conceptualize their training in this way.

S: But if they don't conceptualize it like this, how do they learn to sing?

T: Many singers learn by mimicking other singers. They also rely on comprehensive teaching methods that guide them to feel and control very specific movements in the core. These teaching methods may not reference core muscles—they may reference poetic imagery or spiritual dogma—but they still work to guide the student to feel with detail within the core.

For example, a teacher may want her student to have a free neck for singing. The spine attaches to the skull at the top vertebra called the atlas, at a location approximately between the ears. Freedom of movement at the atlas is important for good singing because the skull must adjust its positioning for different notes, pitches, and emotional states. Additionally, a delicate musculature exists around this spine-to-skull attachment. Small muscles in the upper neck, within the ears, and at the back of the mouth must be flexible and responsive for an expressive voice. So, a teacher will try to guide her student to feel free and flexible where the spine attaches to the skull, but instead of giving an explanation of the musculature involved, the teacher may ask her student to imagine a small balloon between the ears.

Try that. Take your awareness between your ears, feeling the flesh that forms the spaces of the inner ear. Now take your awareness to the back of the neck, relaxing those muscles as needed to feel buoyant like a balloon. Finally, take your awareness to the back of your mouth. Feel the dome of the soft palate and the back of the throat. It's possible to move these small muscles to create an expanded space in the back of the mouth. Now imagine a balloon at the atlas, small, spacious, and light, and feel a freely moving skull on your spine.

S: That feels really good, actually. It makes me wonder, though. If those methods of imagery work, why do we need new theory?

T: Let's step back and put this into perspective. Some people have great talent for feeling and moving in the core. They have the potential to develop their core with sophistication and intelligence, but they also need conceptual guidance to understand how it works. We now live at a time when people want to understand their deepest felt experiences in scientific terms. The question is, how do we approach it?

The muscles are part of a sensory system, though it can be difficult to conceptualize muscles in this way. Conceptualizing the other senses isn't very difficult. It's obvious that the eyes are the sensory terrain for sight. When we close our eyes, we stop seeing what is in front of us. It's obvious that something touching the skin creates sensation.

The concept of muscles feeling, on the other hand, is a much trickier subject. The muscles reside beneath the skin and have no air contact with the outside world, which can make us assume that muscles don't perceive changes occurring outside the body. Actually, muscles feel many sensations initiated outside the body. A person receiving a massage feels sensations of tension, pain, release, and relaxation in the muscles. Muscles also feel forces of physics like temperature, gravity, and air pressure. Additionally, muscles feel changes in the environment inside the body: changes in circulation, hormone activity, nutrition, and their own movement sensations.

Our muscles are very sensitive to these forces and experiences occurring outside and inside the body, but it's taken people thousands of years to understand the forces themselves. Without understanding the forces, people couldn't approach the felt experience. This created a split in the study of felt experience as it did with the chakras: experience exists without the theory of the forces to explain it, so a religious or spiritual explanation takes that place. These conceptualizations of inner experience have worked for centuries for people with limited knowledge about the core, and even today, they continue to work for all kinds of people. For singers they work in an imagistic way. But the dogma and images don't reflect the real truth, which more people are beginning to realize.

In essence, we're now at a unique point in time when many people want to understand the truth of their core experience, but they don't want to understand it with religion, spiritual dogma, or imagery. As the vocabularies that accompany these abstractions continue to be theoretically disproved by science, people search for new ways to explain their experiences with theory that is consistent with the biology of the body. This kind of inquiry pushes fast for a change in paradigm, where we must revisit felt experience in its rawest form, and from there, reform our concepts for what we feel.

S: Is there a soul?

T: There is an experience of a soul.

S: But the soul isn't real?

T: What do you think?

S: It doesn't make scientific sense, but I wonder about it because I have experiences that move me, and I can't explain them. It can't just be all in my head. I feel there is something more.

T: What do you think of the idea that the soul is not real, but the soul experience is real?

S: But what would cause the soul experience?

T: To answer that question, we have to examine the soul experience as it is felt in the body. Let's create an experience where we explore the soul as if it were a real substance. Let yourself relax into the subtler sensations of the body. Gently feel your breath movement low in the pelvis. Feel the sensation of movement in the lower back, belly, then up around the ribs. Bring awareness to your chest, your neck, and head. Now imagine the soul as a spiritual substance within you. Describe the soul to me. Allow that felt conceptualization to inspire a description of the soul and say whatever comes to your mind.

S: Okay. The soul is the part of me that is pure. It's my eternal self. It existed before my body and will be there after I die.

T: So, your body houses your soul.

S: Yes, I have to take care of my body to keep the soul.

T: And when your body dies?

S: Well, the soul supposedly would go somewhere else.

T: Does your soul influence what you say and do?

S: Yeah. My soul expresses itself through my body.

T: How does that work?

S: I don't know.

T: Where is the soul in the body?

S: It's maybe around my heart I suppose.

T: Is it always around your heart?

S: No, because I feel it all throughout my body. I'll feel it below my heart and sometimes lower.

T: Does it move within you?

S: It moves, but not like a little thing that moves around, it's more like it's part of the fabric of my body. Maybe it's not only around my heart. Maybe it's everywhere, but it can move and expand and intensify when it wants.

T: It seems to obey some rules.

S: Well, it needs my body. It's like they have a symbiotic relationship with each other.

T: You said that the soul can move and expand and intensify. How does that affect the muscular body?

S: What do you mean?

T: Let's say you had an experience of love that you felt in your heart. Would there be physical movement, like expansion and intensified feeling in your chest?

S: I guess so, like the chest expanding, and feeling warmth in my heart. It's as if it makes impressions on my heart.

T: It's physical. You are describing something that seems to physically permeate the muscles in the body causing them to move. There are two variables we have to work with: the muscles moving and something moving the muscles.

S: It's really that much about muscles?

T: We experience intimately with our muscles. For example, what is the heart made of?

S: Muscle.

T: We feel sensations in our hearts, and we feel sensations throughout the core. Muscles reside around and inside the head and the neck. They are between each rib, and they stretch around the rib cage. The domed diaphragm under the lungs moves for breath as well as emotions. All of these muscles feel sensations, which include sensations of movement. When we are "moved," our core muscles are moving.

S: Then the soul would have a symbiotic relationship with these muscles, causing them to move and expand and feel.

T: That's the idea. Let's examine the concept of the soul further by going back to the variables in the equation: the muscles that move, and something that moves them. You mentioned that you have experiences that move you. When do you have these experiences?

S: Some of the most meaningful for me are in nature, and it can be anything—a grassy field with a big sky, or I could be in a mossy forest with fog misting the treetops.

T: That sounds beautiful. What do you feel?

S: I feel…the movement of the nature around me. It's subtle, but it's an awareness moving through me.

T: It sounds like you intimately and emotionally experience nature. Many human emotions are defined by human interaction. We read, mimic, and interact with each other's core postures in detail, which is made possible by a common core musculature. Outdoor nature, though, is different. It has no musculature, but it still feeds the senses, and it still moves, like the wind moving through the trees and grasses, or the rain falling. As you experience nature, what kind of core postures do you create within yourself?

S: I don't know. How do you interact with nature in terms of core postures?

T: Try to create a core posture in yourself that mimics the sound and sight of wind moving through the branches of tall trees. What does it feel like?

S: The sound of wind is soft, but it has the potential for power.

T: Where does it feel soft?

S: Around my head, my neck, my chest.

T: And where do you feel power?

S: In my lower body, my gut.

T: And the sight of the trees, what posture does that create?

S: I think a swaying in my upper body, but a rooted feeling in my legs.

T: You created a full-body posture representing the wind moving through the branches of tall trees. It's not only what you see and hear that creates the experience. All the senses influence the forming of the inner experience. As you experience nature, you create an experience within yourself. While the experience forms, the musculature engages in subtle reflex activity; hormones release, movement and sensation is felt, and memories may be recalled or formed. You experience an impression formed by things that are not like you. By empathizing with their form and movement, you create core postures within yourself to feel more like them.

It is a soul experience, with no soul substance moving through you. The soul experience emerges into consciousness as you feel and acknowledge movement and sensation within. The experiences may feel subtle and complex, or raw and powerful depending on the nature you experience and how you experience it. Cultivating these kinds of inner experiences creates a vibrant soul—deep, full-movement experiences very rooted in the physical body. Your muscles are integral to the soul experience because they compose a moving, feeling terrain that can also initiate movement and sensation. You could say that muscles, especially core muscles, are the soul terrain.

S: You're saying the soul is muscle?

T: It's not that simple, but yes, muscles don't get credit as the flesh integral to the soul experience. People have long debated the soul, but they have not yet acknowledged the muscular role.

S: Why?

T: As a culture, we're now beginning to define our deep experiences in terms of the biology of the body—the felt biology of the body. Much of our experiences in the core cannot be readily seen; they can only be felt. Feeling is the tool that gathers the soul experience, and many people, though they experience feelings, do not know how to skillfully feel. Without the skills to analyze inner feelings, some people may embrace more abstract ideas that are readily available and may not inquire into their own flesh. Some may conceptualize a controller of experience, embracing the idea that muscles are always commanded by the brain and the nervous system, for example. Many people in science prefer paradigms that don't demand them to feel with skill. But such paradigms, no matter how entrenched, are not truths.

S: What kind of science do you mean? Are you talking about neuroscience?

T: Neuroscience is a good example. Neuroscience is an exciting field of study, with a flaw: it assumes that the brain controls almost everything, if not everything having to do with emotions, spiritual experience, and mind.

S: That bothers me. Neuroscience seems to think it's all brain to body, but it's not true. It's also body to brain—that dialogue like you said.

T: Neuroscience is doing tremendous work, but philosophically, its brain-to-body paradigm is mistaken. In this age of globalization, when people labor to uncover new links that unite the minds of humanity, we turn to a scientific paradigm that excludes a major variable in the equation: muscles as a sensory terrain for feeling. Muscles have to be recognized for their sensory characteristics. Theories to explain processes of experience—that, in reality, greatly depend on active muscle participation—are being disproportionately theorized as brain and nerve controlled processes.

S: The brain is still important though, right?

T: It's incredibly important, but it works in conjunction with the sensory terrain. No one would deny the eye's role communicating with the brain to generate sight, but people don't yet realize that the core muscles play the same functional role for emotional feeling. Things are changing, though. People are showing a growing interest in the musculature of the body in response to the failures of the brain-to-body paradigm. Understanding that the brain and core work together to create the mind will require a paradigm shift and a change in the type of theorists investigating the truths of inner experience. For the new investigators, intelligent feeling will be a tool to analyze inner experience, and subjective investigation will become a legitimate science for exploring the true nature of the self.

S: How will religion play into this?

T: There are many religious people who can feel with great skill. They have cultivated their ability to feel soulful movement and sensation. However, many are strictly required to reason about their inner experiences with religious dogma. This makes them less open to explaining their experiences in terms of sensory musculature. Religion acknowledges the soul experience, but cannot reconcile spiritual dogma with science. So, between science and religion, a problem has emerged: science can't feel and religion can't reason.

S: Then who is left?

T: People who have the ability to reason through their felt experience, people not satisfied with the scientific paradigms or the religious paradigms, not satisfied but still seeking explanations for the profound experiences they feel. Conceptualizing sensory muscles creates new theoretical tools for understanding the ancient wisdoms of felt experience, but there are some tradeoffs. It's very humbling to conceptualize soul experience as muscle experience. Muscles, after all, are mortal flesh. When the muscles die, the soul experience dies.

S: You're saying there is nothing experienced after we die.

T: That's right. Soul is an experience of the physical body. Our bodies are the soul.

S: What is creativity?

T: Like many of the topics we've discussed, creativity is a process and has no initial source. A continuous dialogue within the body builds the creative experience, but to understand the core's role in creativity, we have to get into the core and analyze specific inner movements.

  Bring attention to your core, head to pelvis, and begin to observe the experience within. We will be moving deep into the body in order to analyze creativity. I want to focus on an experience often integral to creativity, pleasure, specifically a particular core posture of pleasure called the pelvic yawn. It's a fascinating process blending pleasurable pelvic contraction with pleasurable breath movement. The process creates a pleasurable inner pose that structures our core to create and enjoy creating. To explain it, we should break the pelvic yawn into its two main components: the pelvic contraction and the yawn. I want to start with the yawn. Tell me, what do you think about yawning? Is a yawn a pleasant experience?

S: Pleasant? I guess I've never really thought of it as pleasant or unpleasant. When I think of yawning, I think of being tired.

T: When you yawn, what's happening?

S: I'm taking a big ol' breath.

T: Describe the muscle movement when you yawn.

S: It's a big movement. The mouth is wide, the throat stretches, and I take a big breath.

T: That's true, but let's observe more deeply. Here, I'll initiate a yawn. <YAWN> There is movement in the mouth and throat. The mouth opens, the soft palate lifts, the tongue flexes, and the throat lowers. Then, throughout the rest of the core, muscle movement expands the chest and upper back, the diaphragm flattens to inhale, the lower belly and back expand, and within the pelvis, muscles contract and stretch.

S: When you describe it like that, it sounds dramatic.

T: It should. The yawn not only takes a big breath, it also fully stretches the deep core muscles, which feels good.

S: That's interesting. I realized that a yawn feels really refreshing.

T: Would you say a yawn is a pleasant experience?

S: I guess, but I don't really like the word pleasant.

T: What word would you use?

S: The way you were describing it, I might say it's pleasurable.

T: Okay, so a yawn is a pleasurable breath experience.

S: That feels better.

T: Alright. The yawn is pleasurable because it effectively stretches the core musculature into a robust breath. Like all muscles, the core muscles need a robust stretch every once in a while. That's a yawn. It's a natural process that engages and stretches the core muscles. Understanding the nature of the yawn can help you understand how the core muscles dramatically move to breathe. Singers, opera singers especially, capitalize on this movement process. They learn to move into the core posture of a "half-yawn," not the full posture, but a half-expanded posture involving the entire core, head to pelvis. I mention this because I want you to understand that it is possible to re-create a yawn, or a variation of a yawn, by learning to manipulate the core muscles into any core posture. I'll engage it now. Notice that my voice becomes rounder and more articulate.

S: You sound kind of high class British.

T: Yes. Now, I'm going to add extra muscle contraction in my pelvis and low belly, which stimulates inter-core reflexes throughout my body including my face. You can see in my face that the posture is pleasurable.

S: That looks a little orgasmic.

Is There A Soul?

T: I've created a pelvic yawn, though my process was out of order. The most authentic pelvic yawn is actually initiated from the pelvis. A contraction and stretch initiated in the pelvis triggers inter-core reflexes causing a specific kind of a pelvic yawn throughout the core. It combines pelvic contraction with dramatic breath movement, creating a core posture movement of pleasure. From there, it can be further manipulated with muscle contraction to posture a powerful ecstasy. Notice the increased intensity around my eyes.

S: That is intense. I don't think I can do that.

T: It takes training, which you could learn. For now, consider the idea that the creative process engages pleasure, and pleasure engages the pelvic yawn. It feels good. The core muscles feel good—the same core muscles that speak, express, and communicate. By moving the core muscles into a core posture of pleasure, the body inwardly adopts a physical pose for creative activity, whether for thinking, building, singing, or sex. This may be uncomfortable for some people to think about, but we shouldn't be prudish about the creative process. Creativity is pleasurable. It stems from sexuality. The felt experience of the pleasurable pelvic yawn can fuel us to have grand ideas, to create life, and make beautiful things.

S: That reminds me of when I've seen great music performers. Sometimes they seem to go into a kind of ecstasy.

T: What does it look like? Can you describe the core posture?

S: The mouth is open, the eyes might be closed, or open and intense like yours were, and their body seems riveted in music.

T: You describe what you see. Now think about what is felt. The pelvic yawn is a muscular expression of sexual experience with felt sensations inside the head, neck, chest, abdomen, and pelvis. It orchestrates an expression of creativity appropriately initiated from where we create life. A person can engage a robust pelvic yawn which you observed as powerful and ecstatic.

S: That's intense.

T: Yes. But it doesn't always have to be a big expression. Like any core posture, a pelvic yawn can be subpostured for movements of subtle pleasure. A subpostured pelvic yawn can accompany thought for an inner creative experience.

S: So, I could learn how to pelvic yawn to be creative?

T: Yes.

S: How do I learn to do that?

T: First, you need to be confident feeling throughout your core, including within your pelvis. Becoming familiar with your core musculature is essential to creating core postures like the pelvic yawn.

S: That sounds a little scary.

T: Why?

S: It seems strange to know that much about yourself.

T: It's strange because it is intimate and unfamiliar, but it is also your body and your experience. Don't think that there are only certain times to be creative or only certain people who are allowed to be creative. Much of that is society trying to control us or convince us that creativity should be valued only as a product. On the contrary, there is great value in being creatively authentic. Creative authenticity engages a true creative process with unsuppressed sexual movement. We need sexual movement to be creative. Without it our personal expressions become neutered imitations of creativity.

S: Do you mean they're fake?

T: To put it in strict terms of the body, expressions that avoid feeling and engaging from the sexual centers are not creative expressions because the creative process requires sexual movement. The creative process includes pleasure; the pleasure process includes the pelvis yawn; the pelvic yawn process is initiated from the pelvis. To avoid feeling within the pelvis or to suppress the pelvic yawn is to suppress the creative process. To learn how to feel, engage, control, and express the pelvic yawn is to sophisticate the creative process. Accessing your creative process comes not necessarily through sex as much as it is through sexual experience according to your individual nature.

S: I kind of understand what you're saying about being authentically sexual, but it seems that there is already a lot of sex being thrown at us from culture, media especially, and none of that seems to have anything to do with developing personal creativity.

T: That's true. But realize that people obtain power by controlling or suppressing other people's creativity. One way to control creativity is to control sexuality. The media does this on a mass scale, distributing ideas about how we should be sexual. Intelligently creative people, however, challenge those controls by developing an inner awareness of themselves, and by being inwardly aware, they are more apt to maneuver out of the controls of culture.

S: I get that. I want to escape the controls of culture. So, let's say I develop an inner awareness and maneuver out of the controls, then what do I do?

T: Be courageous. Work toward fully realizing your creative self. Then you can creatively work toward remaking the culture.

S: What is language?

T: Language begins as the muscular communication of experience. Muscles speak and gesture language. Spoken language is preceded with an inhalation. We inhale, then during the exhalation, the core muscles move through core postures to form words and emotions.

S: You mean air moves through the vocal cords and the mouth while they move to form words.

T: That's not entirely it. Words are made up of vowels and consonants, all of which have their own core postures, and core postures engage the core musculature from head to pelvis.

S: Really? I get that vowels and consonants change the shape of the mouth and vocal cords, but there isn't anything going on below the neck, is there?

T: Actually, there is. Try putting your hand on your belly and say the word "key" with a hard "k" sound.

S: "Key." My belly contracts.

T: Yes, inter-core reflexes coordinate the core posture so all the muscles move together.

S: But if I say it quietly, "key," I don't feel it in my belly.

T: The quieter you say it, the closer you get to subposturing the word. You might not feel it, but there will be some contraction—perhaps not as much in the belly but definitely in the diaphragm. Let's try another word. Take the word "pain" and divide it into its consonants and vowels, starting with the "p" consonant. Where is the contraction in the body?

S: <puh> It's in the lips and in the belly.

T: Now the "ā" vowel in pain.

S: <ā>It's in the mouth, the tongue.

T: Just in the mouth? Say it louder.

S: <Ā> Okay I feel contraction in my face and the belly, too.

T: Now for the "n" consonant.

S: <n> That's a little nasally. <n> And it's also in the throat and belly.

T: Excellent, well-mapped, especially when you picked up that there is more vibration in the throat for the "n." That's very good. Consider that you move through those core postures in one breath to say the word "pain."

S: Pain. Okay, I get that. I'm moving through a series of core postures now in one exhalation to say this sentence.

T: That's right. Core postures create every vowel and consonant. Of course speaking involves more than producing vowels and consonants. Speech blends core postures of vowels and consonants with core postures of emotion and tonal pitch. Postural blending happens continually in the core. Imagine a kind of movable architecture, shifting and shaping to form combinations of core postures. For example, say person is in pain. Pain itself has a core posture. The event of pain immediately triggers a reflexive contraction of the core musculature. So, blending the word "pain" with the core posture of pain creates an authentic spoken expression. The word sounds authentic because the vowels and consonants are blended with a core posture of pain.

S: The word "pain" needs the core posture to be authentic?

T: That's right. The core posture of pain came first, the word followed. The core posture holds more meaning than the word. This isn't to say that words are not important. In fact, saying the word "pain" could potentially trigger a remembered experience of pain. Still, the remembered experience has a physical structure. Pain has a core posture. Without the core posture, the word becomes meaningless.

S: What about people who say something different than what they're feeling? How would it work if a person said, "I'm fine," but you could hear pain in their voice?

T: Do you mean, how can we choose to speak words that don't match the inner experience?

S: Yeah.

T: That explanation goes deeper into the theories of thought that we touched on before. It has to do with how we alternate between robust core postures and subtle core postures, in other words, moving between core postures that other people see and hear, and the subpostures that people can't see and hear. A person can subposture through an imagined scenario before speaking out loud. The scenario that you mentioned, being in pain but saying, "I'm fine," points to how the core muscles can subposture words and emotions while other events happen in the core.

Let's imagine a scenario: a person is in pain from a stomach ache, but in feeling the pain she quickly imagines other people seeing her posture pain. She subpostures their reaction, making her feel embarrassed, which inwardly motivates her to say something that would make others believe she is not in pain. Then she says "I'm fine" to prevent embarrassment. She subpostured through the experience she wanted to have before saying anything out loud.

S: But that "thought" experience was an actual experience?

T: Yes. Thought subpostures emotions. Think of quiet people feeling like they aren't so quiet.

S: It's like she created an alternate reality within herself.

T: Interesting way to put it. Yes, thinking includes physical activity in the core. When we think, we subposture emotions and we also subvocalize words.

S: Subvocalize?

T: I specifically use the term subvocalization when talking about subposturing words only. Subvocalization is a type of subposturing. It's the act of forming subtle words. Subvocalization tends to engage muscles higher in the core, mainly involving the muscles we need to speak like the tongue, the vocal cords and other muscles throughout the head, neck, and upper torso. We subvocalize words and we subposture emotions. It's important to know that we do both.

S: Because thinking the word is different than feeling the core posture?

T: Exactly. A word represents an experience. The experience includes a core posture. Let's apply this idea to thought. Tell me which is more authentic: the subvocalized word "pain" or the subpostured experience?

S: The subpostured experience is more authentic, but I don't quite understand what that means.

T: When we think, we tend to place more importance on the word than the experience. This can become problematic when trying to understand the nature of thought. We talk to ourselves giving more attention to the words we subvocalize instead of giving attention the experiences we subposture. Yes, words are important. Words have the power to prompt the experience of the word, but without the experience, the word becomes meaningless. For this reason, our self-talk can feel empty. It becomes meaningless when we subvocalize words without feeling the experience.

S: You said that people talk to themselves, and their self-talk can become empty. I understand that, but I don't understand why we do it so much.

T: We all need a range of inner experiences. If you observe people, many people need to talk or emote, but it's not always socially appropriate or they may not have anyone to talk to, so they subposture emotions and subvocalize words to create inner experiences. They satisfy their core needs by creating experiences within themselves.

S: Why do we need so many inner experiences?

T: It's natural for our core muscles to move and feel. Our core muscles form a sensory terrain evolved to interact with the world both outside and inside the body. Core muscles enable us to experience the external world within ourselves. We need this interaction. We need to move and be moved. How the core specifically needs to move depends on a person's individual needs, but in general, everyone needs inner experiences. This is one reason our core muscles are often continuously moving, sometimes robustly, sometimes subtly, posturing, subposturing, subvocalizing, and feeling.

S: Doesn't that get tiring?

T: You're starting to feel tired.

S: This is a lot to think about.

T: It's true. Core muscles can get very tired from everything they do. Like any muscle of the body, core muscles need rest, too.

Is There A Soul?

S: How does meditation work?

T: Have you done much meditation?

S: A little. I did a meditation retreat a year ago.

T: What was that like?

S: It was intense. It was ten days. The first three days, we focused awareness on a little spot under the nose, feeling the breath move over the skin. The idea was to learn how to feel sensations in a tiny area. After those three days, we were asked to slowly pass our awareness over the entire body, paying close attention to detailed sensations.

T: What did you think of it?

S: It was one of the hardest things I've ever done. I'm pretty disciplined, but meditating ten hours a day is not easy. We also practiced noble silence, so we didn't talk. Though there were some good moments, too. I remember when I was able to completely observe my breath as if I was watching an animal breathe, but my eyes were closed and there were no images. I remember going for a walk and feeling captivated by the sound of the wind in the trees.

T: It sounds like you trained subtle sensory awareness and then experienced simple things in a new way.

S: Yeah, it was really amazing.

T: But?

S: But I still don't really get a lot of it. The philosophy still doesn't make sense to me. I get that meditation is supposed to quiet the mind, but during the retreat, I was in so much pain sitting there. It really hurt.

T: Your muscles?

S: They were screaming to move. It seems weird or unnatural to make them sit there and do nothing. How is meditation supposed to solve that?

T: How did they teach you to quiet the mind?

S: They said to feel the sensations of the skin, and when the mind wandered, to gently bring it back to the skin. Just observe, not react. Patiently and persistently realize that sensations were rising and passing away, changing.

T: What do you think that meant?

S: I guess there were two things happening. I was trying to focus on the sensations of the skin, but my mind was going bonkers. I had movie dialogue going through my head. I had imaginary conversations with people. We were supposed to notice what the mind was doing, but not judge it. The goal seemed to be to quiet the mind, but I don't know what that means.

T: Try to analyze your mind experience in terms of subpostures.

S: You're saying that my mind wanted to create subpostures?

T: No, your mind was subposturing.

S: So, my core muscles were still moving while I was meditating?

T: Yes, your core muscles were still in conversation with the brain.

S: That's a funny way to put it, but I guess it's possible that there would be a lot of core activity even if you are sitting there with your eyes closed.

T: The meditation setting focused your attention to feel the activity of the core.

S: Man, I sure felt it. Why couldn't everything relax?

T: That's the right question to ask. That's exactly what you do to quiet the mind.

S: What do you mean? Just relax?

T: Not quite. Your instructions were to not react, which can be a little misleading. Really what they are saying is to do everything you can to keep the core muscles relaxed. Continuously relax the muscles to dissipate all core postures, all subpostures, all subvocalization.

S: I don't get it.

T: What would it mean to relax the core posture of anger?

S: The core posture of anger is in the front of the body, so I would relax the core posture by relaxing the muscles?

T: Yes. You would feel the core posture of anger in all of its locations throughout the core then bring your attention to each location relaxing the muscles.

S: I get that, but emotions aren't only about muscles, right? Hormones are involved, too, and well, you can't relax hormones.

T: Hormones do stimulate core postures, but remember that core postures also stimulate hormone activity. For example, moving into the core posture of anger could stimulate the brain to trigger hormone activity back to where anger is initiated, which is something that could take a subposture of anger into a more expressed posture of anger. Both hormones and core postures continuously influence each other, creating a cycle, core postures stimulating hormones stimulating core postures. By relaxing the core postures you are breaking the cycle.

S: But the hormones are still there, right? If I all of a sudden get a rush of hormones, I can't get rid of them.

T: That's when you observe how your muscles feel while continuing to relax them.

S: Wait, I am relaxing first, and then what?

T: Then observe the inner environment of the body simply by feeling it; feel impressions on your relaxed muscles. This is how you quiet the mind. By relaxing the core muscles, you dissipate the subpostures of emotion and subvocalization, and then the mind relaxes.

S: How do you relax subvocalization?

T: Relax the muscles that subvocalize. Try it now. Relax your tongue. Feel from the tip, over the top to the very back of the tongue within the throat. Relax the sides of the tongue. The tongue is just one subvocalizing muscle. Relax the muscles of the jaw, the mouth, the throat, the lips. It's very possible to learn how to relax these small, speaking muscles. Having a self-knowledge of your subvocalizing muscles will allow you to understand the nature of your subvocalizing self, which is essential if you want to learn how to quiet it.

S: No wonder it was so hard. Let's say I learn to relax all my subpostures of emotion and subvocalization, then what?

T: Then there is only the felt movement of peaceful breath.

S: What is consciousness?

T: What kind of consciousness?

S: There are different kinds?

T: There is a spectrum of consciousness ranging from awareness of the world around you to being aware of your thinking self.

S: That's the one I mean, awareness of myself.

T: To understand it, you have to approach it as a process.

S: What's the process?

T: It's a process of acknowledging experience.

S: How would you acknowledge it?

T: By experiencing something, subtly replaying it, and then attaching a core posture to that replayed experience.

S: What do you mean? Why would I do that?

T: As we go through life, we continually have inner-felt experiences. Sometimes life events can be complicated or overwhelming, so we manage by taking a group of felt experiences, replaying them in our mind, and then assigning the group a single core posture. It acknowledges the entire experience and simplifies it emotionally. For example, "yes" is a word, but it also a core posture. We replay an experience and feel the pleasurable core posture of "yes" after replaying it.

S: That's really different. The idea of "yes" being a pleasurable core posture is really different.

T: Then let's start with the experience of "yes." Before we understand it as a word, we feel it as a process of the core.

S: What do you mean "before we understand it as a word"?

T: I mean before we learn to speak. A baby will experience the core posture of "yes" before she will learn the word "yes" or "da" or "oui" or all the other ways that people throughout the world say yes. It is first experienced as a distinct core posture.

S: What's the core posture for "yes"?

T: Do you remember the yawn? We talked about a yawn as a pleasurable breath. Some variations of yawn movement can become very subtle. With this in mind, I want you to imagine posturing a subtle yawn. Not the full posture, a subtle contraction of the musculature in the back of the core to form the core posture of "yes." I say the back of the core because the back half of the diaphragm commands more movement than the front. The diaphragm is shaped like an upside-down bowl under the lungs but not a round bowl. It's more like a kidney shape with its two ends on either side of the spine. Two times the surface area resides in the back half of the diaphragm than in the front. Therefore a yawn—being a full contraction of the diaphragm—engages a great deal of diaphragmatic movement in the back of the body. The movement is not just limited to the diaphragm. Muscles stretch in the back of the throat, the soft palate rises, and further down the body, the low back expands, as does the pelvic floor.

S: I'm yawning as you describe it.

T: What this all points to is a satisfying, pleasurable breath that involves considerable core muscle movement in the back of the core. "Yes" is a variation of this movement. The core posture of "yes" engages the breath musculature in a way that feels good.

S: If that's "yes" then what's "no"?

T: The core posture of "no" is a process of contraction that stops the breath. Its pattern of contraction is primarily at the front of the core. The core posture of "yes" encourages a breath, and the core posture of "no" stops it. They are two distinctly different felt experiences. This is important to understand because we live by our felt experiences. Our core musculature feels and moves through vital processes. Breathing is a continuous and essential movement in the core. To stop the breath is to deny the essential, whereas efficiently moving the muscles to breathe optimizes the essential. Therefore, the core postures of "yes" and "no" are effective tools for connecting the rightness of something or the wrongness of something to an actual felt experience. For example, think of interacting with kids. Children need to feel "yes" and "no" in order to learn how to behave.

S: How do little kids learn the core postures of "yes" and "no"?

T: The core postures are demonstrated to kids over and over until they learn to repeat them.

S: You're talking about how a parent tells the kid "yes" and "no" all the time?

T: The parent says the words "yes" and "no" blended with the corresponding core postures of "yes" and "no." The core postures are more important than the words, after all, many words can represent the core postures of "yes" and "no."

S: Si. I understand when you say the core posture is more important than the word.

T: Ya. The words "yes" and "no" are meaningless if they are not blended with their respective core postures.

S: Okay. That makes sense.

T: Good. Now that you understand the core postures of "yes" and "no," try to imagine them acknowledging one's own thoughts as a way to organize the thought experience.

S: Acknowledging one's own thoughts? What do you mean, don't we do that already?

T: I mentioned before that as we go through life, we continuously have inner-felt experiences. Some happen as we experience the world outside us, but some experiences we create ourselves with our imagination. After an imagination experience, we learn to acknowledge it by assigning it a single core posture.

S: I'm not sure what you mean by the imagination experience.

T: I'm talking about any thought experience. As children, we learn how to think. Let's go through an example between a child and an adult, using simple math. Here's the scenario: I ask a child, "What is two plus two?" The child thinks. As she thinks, her core movement becomes subtle and focused. Then she says, "four," and I say, "yes," and then the child engages the "yes" core posture. The child is learning how to think by learning how to acknowledge her experience. In this case, she acknowledges it with the core posture of "yes," which feels good.

S: It's like a little reward?

T: Yes. It is a pleasurable experience that the child is encouraged to feel after giving the right answer.

S: If the kid answers with "five" instead of "four," then you would say "no," which would tell the kid to stop her breath?

T: Yes.

S: That's not very nice.

T: It works. It's a way to punctuate an experience with another experience that feels good or feels bad in order to acknowledge the experience as good or bad.

S: Is it always that black and white?

T: No. The core postures of "yes" and "no" are very clear examples that I am using to show how we acknowledge experience. The core postures of pleasure, love, anger, or sadness could acknowledge an experience. There are even variations of the core postures of "yes" and "no," but for the sake of defining consciousness, we should stick to "yes" and "no" in order to clearly define the process.

S: Okay.

T: We started with a scenario where an adult acknowledges a child's experience with core postures of "yes" and "no." Now we will explore the idea that we learn to acknowledge our own thoughts with the subtle core postures of "yes" and "no." When we think, we don't necessarily use the words "yes" and "no," but we engage their core postures. For example, you might be thinking through a problem, and after a while you may come to an answer that makes sense. After you come to that answer, you would acknowledge your efforts by subposturing a "yes."

S: Just the subposture? You mean without subvocalizing the word "yes"?

T: That's exactly right. You subposture "yes" without subvocalizing the word "yes." The core posture and the word are two different movement processes. Understanding the difference brings us closer to understanding consciousness.

I said before that consciousness is a process of acknowledging experience. You experience something and then subtly replay the experience, then acknowledge it with a core posture. This process of replaying experience can be relatively simple, like remembering a food that tasted good, or it can become more complex as the topics of thought become more complex. You might think about another person and try to decide how you feel about him. You imagine past experiences with this person; you imagine potential experiences with this person. Let's say these imagined experiences make you feel good, so you begin acknowledging your imagined experiences with the posture of "yes." By acknowledging an elaborate process with a simple core posture, you establish a felt "point of view." You begin to associate the person with your pleasurable core posture of "yes."

S: That's a process of consciousness?

T: It's part of the ever-moving stream of consciousness. We continuously experience life, re-experience it through thought, and then acknowledge these inner experiences. We become conscious of the thinking self when we become aware of that entire process, and acknowledge it. In essence, consciousness of the thinking self is the act of acknowledging our ability to acknowledge thought experience. And again, we acknowledge it with a variety of core postures including the core postures of "yes" or "no."

S: That means we need core postures to be conscious of the thinking self.

T: Which makes our core musculature vital to our becoming conscious of the thinking self.

S: If we didn't have core muscles, we wouldn't be conscious?

T: That's right. Our core muscles intelligently feel and move in order to shape and reshape our consciousness.

S: What would a modern spirituality be?

T: Why do you think we need a modern spirituality?

S: It seems to me, like you say, religious dogma doesn't work anymore. We have access to information about all kinds of religions and spiritualties all over the world, but to me, it's not about which religion is right and which is wrong. It's about finding a deeper truth. I want a new way to experience and understand who we are. I want to understand the spiritual nature of ourselves.

T: Do you need spiritual experiences?

S: Definitely.

T: How do you imagine ideal spirituality in your life?

S: I want it to be part of a functional society. I would like some community. I don't want to have to take drugs to have a spiritual experience or believe in something that I don't think is there. Is that possible?

T: It's a good question. What do you think religion gives to people when it comes to spiritual experience?

S: It gives them a place to practice their faith. It gives them dogma. I'm not sure beyond that.

T: Let's start with analyzing a church experience. Say a person goes to church. All around him are religious symbols, architecture, music, and art. Rituals and remembered ways of behaving guide the service. What's the purpose of having all of that in church?

S: I think he would say to express his faith.

Is There A Soul?

T: What would you say?

S: I would say it's to create an experience.

T: What kind of experience?

S: A deep emotional experience. I just realized how true that is—that church gives people an elaborate emotional experience.

T: What does that mean to you?

S: It's weird. It means that people need help to feel deeply. It's like they can't do it by themselves, so they go to church, which orchestrates a ritual to move people through deeper emotions. I don't judge that. It makes sense, but I don't agree with the dogma in church, so I don't go, but I need help sometimes too.

T: Help moving through deep emotions?

S: And expressing them. I would like to feel and hear and see more wisdom around me to guide me through deeper truths.

T: What do you think is keeping that from happening?

S: I've been thinking about this a lot. Honestly, I don't think people have a vocabulary to talk about deep experience without referencing religion.

T: In many ways religion is very effective helping people move through their deep experiences. Deep experiences can be very powerful and overwhelming. Suffering, love, ecstasy, injury, and fear are powerful core experiences that can overwhelm us. We need help moving through, calming, expressing, and structuring these experiences. For many people, religion fulfills that need for inner guidance. For example, a person may go to church when she feels sad over the loss of a loved one. Church creates an environment that helps her express and understand her experience. She feels better, but her participation is contingent on reasoning about her experiences with religious dogma. Dogma becomes real for people when their felt religious experiences are real. They feel moved, comforted, changed, and awakened. A religious culture that can help people structure their inner experiences is very powerful. After all, how we feel in our core influences how we think and act.

S: That's interesting. It seems like people need community and they need spiritual structure. I feel that there is a lot truth to many spiritualities, but there are so many to choose from. I don't want to reject everything, but I don't want to embrace everything either.

T: There is much wisdom in many religions and spiritualties. We can still connect to it, but many of the ancient wisdoms need modern explanations. The explanations will come when people venture into their bodies with the intention of defining their spiritual experiences as muscular experiences of the core.

S: Is it possible to do that on my own?

T: Yes. Still, everyone needs support.

S: I definitely need support. I'd like to have people around me asking the same questions and helping me understand my inner experiences.

T: It's possible that people will begin working together to understand inner experience in terms of the core musculature. It could potentially lay the foundation for a modern spirituality, replacing the ideas of spirit with the understanding of a sense.

Is There A Soul?

S: What makes a person wise?

T: A wise person has learned to intelligently feel and move with the nature of their core.

S: How would you learn to do that?

T: It involves training how to feel.

S: Do you mean something like meditation?

T: There would be meditative aspects to the training, and there would be athletic aspects as well.

S: Athletic. Do you mean muscular training in the core? How would that be trained?

T: It would start with coordinating big, almost exaggerated movements within the core. To explain, let's get out of the core for a second. I'll give an example that might be easier to conceptualize: learning to walk. Walking requires complex coordinated movement of the body. Think about a young child who is taking her first steps. Young children, when they first learn to walk, make big awkward movements with their bodies.

S: That's true. They pretty much have to go for it and mess up and go for it again.

T: That's a good way to put it.

S: The awkward part really makes sense.

T: Why?

S: It has to be awkward at first because how else is the kid going to learn?

T: Explain more.

S: It's not as if kids take each body part and work on it individually before putting it all together, right? A kid can't learn to balance on one leg, make it perfect, work on the other leg, make it perfect, and then walk perfectly.

T: We agree that the basic movement of walking has to work before it can become more efficient, and that initial process is awkward and messy.

S: That makes sense.

T: It is the same for developing wisdom.

S: What does that mean?

T: It means that a person has to move awkwardly within the core as part of the training to become wise.

S: You have to go for it.

T: You have to be willing to robustly express a range of core postures.

S: By a range of core postures do you mean an emotional range?

T: That's part of it, yes.

S: What kind of range? Which emotions would be included in the training?

T: All of them.

S: Oh. So, that includes the not-so-favored ones like sadness and anger?

T: Yes. It's important to know how to feel and engage a range of emotions without suppression.

S: Does that mean that wisdom can't be developed if certain core postures are suppressed?

T: That's right.

S: It sounds so physical.

T: It is. Developing wisdom is a physical endeavor.

S: I'm still confused. Don't we learn to feel all the core postures at some point? We have words for all emotions, so doesn't that mean we've developed our range?

T: Those are good questions. Though we experience a wide range of core postures when we are younger, as we get older we lose the opportunity and the ability to express a range of core postures. As a result we start valuing one emotion over another, one process of core movement over another, and in doing that, we replace a range of emotional states with a few dominant core postures.

S: Some emotional core postures are overused and others aren't used at all.

T: Even though most adults know the words and have memories of a range of emotions, most can't robustly and intelligently express them.

S: I bet adults who can are good actors.

T: Good actors refine a range of core postures.

S: When people overuse a few emotions and suppress others, it might make them seem fake, right? Like some people try to smile all the time. Drives me nuts.

T: Why do they bother you?

S: It just doesn't seem natural. Really, you can't be that happy all the time.

T: I agree, but go deeper into explaining why. Think about core postures.

S: Okay, if a person makes it a point to be smiling all the time, they're just engaging in one core posture, right?

T: Go on.

S: I think about standing or sitting in one position for a long time, and how the muscles get tired.

T: Or tense.

S: Exactly! I can think of a few people who seem tense in their happiness. It's like the muscles have been over-worked into that core posture of "happy."

T: I think you have exposed a truth about people and their pursuit of happiness.

S: Yeah. People push it way too far, and it's not even that I think people are completely faking happiness.

T: Possibly they are very skilled at engaging the "happy" core posture.

S: That's a funny way to think about it. What is the core posture of "happy" anyway?

T: Let's define the core posture of a smile. Engage only the corners of your mouth into a smile while relaxing from the neck down.

S: A fake smile, right? How do I look?

T: Perfect. Now inhale and engage the muscles of your outer ribs, and then around your lower torso and back…and smile with your mouth and eyes.

S: That does feel more authentic. It feels like an expanded core posture, especially on the sides of my ribs. That's the core posture of smiling?

T: Yes.

S: So, people make it a goal to engage that core posture all the time?

T: Some people do.

S: It's funny how physical it is. What's crazy is that people seem to do it competitively, pushing the happy core posture to bring them status. The tradeoff seems to be a lack of emotional range—a lack of wisdom.

T: Part of being wise is having the ability to move skillfully through a range of core postures as it is necessary. It takes training as well as experience. A wise person not only moves intelligently with the nature of herself, she can skillfully empathize with a range of core postures and emotional states of others. She can also act with appropriately trained core posture movement in a variety of circumstances.

S: How does a person become skilled at creating core postures?

T: Think about the kinds of people who are already skilled at creating core postures.

S: We mentioned actors and singers. Singers are able to move the voice and language in really powerful ways.

T: The most skilled artists understand a wide range of raw emotion, and they understand how to sculpt those raw emotions into sophisticated expressions.

S: Artists can be amazing, but I'm a little confused. Are they necessarily wise? The arts seem more about marketing and entertainment. I'm less inclined to associate wisdom with the arts because artists and musicians and especially patrons seem to focus on the arts as a product to be sold.

T: I think you're right. The culture has moved that way, but that doesn't eliminate the fact that a lot of training is involved to become a skilled artist. Artists spend years refining the dialogue between brain and core to ultimately create that product.

S: Do artists value that training?

T: Some do. Though many, as you pointed out, only value the technique as a means to create a product.

S: Then we should value the technique more.

T: Yes. We should give it recognition. The idea of a product without a mechanism to create it is a false concept. It's like a person believing that there is no mechanism to create electric light. A person with no concept of electricity might explain an electric light using terms referencing magic. In the same way, a person with no concept of sensory core muscles might explain a singer's beautiful voice using terms referencing religion. My point is, the felt mechanisms of the core are still a mystery to people. Only when we start conceptualizing felt experiences as sensory events of the core musculature will we begin penetrating the mystery. You are asking questions at an exciting and confusing time when paradigms are shifting.

S: It does feel confusing, but I also feel like there is a kind of urgency, an excitement for creating something new. I think my problem is organizing myself. How do I figure out how I fit into things?

T: This kind of inquiry is unexplored territory. It's exploration of the self, contingent on self-exploration. You have potential. You have a good sense of feeling, and you're smart. There's potential in you to sophisticate your core muscles. Achieving it takes a certain type of training—a cultivation of the core according to your nature. If you want advice, be courageous. Learn how to intelligently feel and move within your core by pursuing what fulfills you. As you experience within, continuously acknowledge your self-discoveries in sensory terms. By then, you will already be creating something new.

ABOUT THE AUTHOR

Madeline McNeill became a philosopher after years of both formal and autodidactic study. She has a BA in music from Western Washington University. She's participated in the EPCASO (Ezio Pinza Council for American Singers of Opera) program in Italy and two Vipassana meditation retreats. She creates theory with an intense focus on the body, integrating her studies in the sciences, arts, music, and world religions with her training in meditation, yoga, and massage. She performs and busks in Spokane, Washington.